COLOR ME SCIENCE

Children's Press
An Imprint of Scholastic Inc.
New York Toronto London Auckland Sydney
Mexico City   New Delhi   Hong Kong
Danbury, Connecticut

Book production: Educational Reference Publishing

Book design: Nancy Hamlen D'Ambrosio

Science adviser: Jennifer A. Roth, M.A.

.

Library of Congress Cataloging-in-Publication Data

Color Me Science.
     p. cm. — (Experiment with science)
  Includes bibliographical references and index.
ISBN-13: 978-0-531-18541-4 (lib. bdg.)   978-0-531-18758-6 (pbk.)
ISBN-10: 0-531-18541-9 (lib. bdg.)   0-531-18758-6 (pbk.)
  1. Color—Juvenile literature. 2. Senses and
sensation—Experiments—Juvenile literature. I. Title. II. Series.
  QC495.5.C62 2008
  535.6—dc22
                              2007014449

No part of this publication may be reproduced in whole or in part, or stored in a retrieval system, or transmitted in any form or by any means, electronic, mechanical, photocopying, recording, or otherwise, without written permission of the publisher. For information regarding permission, write to Scholastic Inc., 557 Broadway, New York, NY 10012.

© 2008 Scholastic Inc.

All rights reserved. Published by Children's Press, an imprint of Scholastic Inc. Printed in the United States of America.

SCHOLASTIC, CHILDREN'S PRESS, and associated logos are trademarks and/or registered trademarks of Scholastic Inc.

1 2 3 4 5 6 7 8 9 10 R   17 16 15 14 13 12 11 10 09 08

CONTENTS

COLOR ME SCIENCE

Our world is filled with color: a bright blue sky, red stop signs, yellow bananas, **green grass. Color is all around us. But what is it?**

Color is how we see light. And light is made of waves. Each of these waves has a different length, called a wavelength. We see each different wavelength as a different color. Sunlight contains all the different wavelengths, or colors, together, so it appears colorless, or white.

Each experiment in this book leads you through the steps you must take to reach a successful conclusion based on scientific results. There are also important symbols you should recognize before you begin your experiment. Here's how the experiments are organized:

Name of experiment

Goal, or purpose, of the experiment

A **You Will Need** box provides a list of supplies you'll need to complete the experiment, as well as the approximate amount of time the experiment should take.

Here's What You Will Do gives step-by-step instructions for working through the experiment.

Here's What's Happening explains the science behind the experiment—and what the conclusion should be.

Mess Factor shows you on a scale of 0 to 5 just how messy the experiment might be (a good thing to know before you begin!).

MESS FACTOR: 3

Science Safety: Whenever you see this caution symbol, read the instructions and be extra careful.

But when a ray of sunlight passes through a raindrop, the light spreads out into all of its different wavelengths. This is when we see a rainbow—and the full range, or spectrum, of colors that make up light.

The experiments in this book will help you understand what color is and why it is important. You'll do experiments that bend light, spread white light into many colors, break colors into more colors, and show you that insects are attracted to certain colors. You'll even see how color is used as a form of natural camouflage! So grab your lab coat, fire up your curiosity, and let's EXPERIMENT WITH SCIENCE!

This symbol means that you should ask an adult to help you or be nearby as you conduct the experiment. Although all the experiments in this book are appropriate and safe for kids to do, whenever you're handling anything that might be sharp or hot, it's important to have adult supervision.

In the back of the book, **Find Out More** offers suggestions of other books to read on the subject of color, and cool Web sites to check out. The **Glossary** (pages 30-31) provides definitions of the highlighted words appearing throughout this book. Finally, the **Index** is the place to go to find exactly what you're looking for.

Here are some important tips before you begin your experiment:

- Check with an adult.
- Read the experiment all the way through.
- Gather everything you need.
- Choose and prepare your "lab" work area.
- Wash and dry your hands.
- Use only clean containers for your experiments.
- Keep careful notes of everything you do and see.
- Stop and ask an adult if you aren't sure what to do.
- When you're finished, clean up your work area completely, and wash your hands!

iT'S A BUG'S CHOiCE

IN THIS WARM-WEATHER EXPERIMENT, YOU'LL FIND OUT WHY BEES AND OTHER **INSECTS** ARE ATTRACTED TO BRIGHT, BEAUTIFUL FLOWERS. AND YOU'LL **COAX** INSECTS INTO REVEALING THEIR FAVORITE COLORS!

YOU WiLL NEED

- ❑ warm, sunny day
- ❑ notebook
- ❑ pen or pencil
- ❑ construction paper—4 sheets in different colors
- ❑ small stones

TIME: 45 MINUTES

MESS FACTOR: 0

The honeybee is attracted to this bright yellow flower. As the bee gathers nectar, bits of pollen from the flower stick to its body.

HERE'S WHAT YOU WILL DO

1 In your notebook, write the names of insects found in your neighborhood down the left margin (perhaps flies, bees, butterflies, ants, and "other"). Write the colors of your construction paper across the top (red, green, yellow, blue).

2 Place the colored papers on a patch of grass, ideally near some flowering plants. A few stones on the corners of each paper will keep them from blowing away.

3 Stand a couple of feet away and keep as still as possible. Watch for arriving insects. In your notebook, make a mark each time a certain kind of insect lands on a colored piece of construction paper.

HERE'S WHAT'S HAPPENING

Flowers need insects for pollination. Pollination is the transfer of pollen from one flower or plant to another. Certain insects are attracted to colors that they associate with their favorite nectar. As they crawl about gathering up the nectar, their bodies become covered with sticky pollen grains. When they land on another flower, their bodies transfer the pollen to that flower.

HOT OR COLD? BLACK OR WHITE?

IN THIS EXPERIMENT, YOU'LL SEE THE EFFECT THAT LIGHT- AND DARK-COLORED FABRICS HAVE ON TEMPERATURE.

YOU WILL NEED

- ❏ a sunny day
- ❏ two thermometers
- ❏ small piece of white fuzzy fabric
- ❏ small piece of black fuzzy fabric
- ❏ clear tape

TIME: 1-1/2 HOURS

MESS FACTOR: 0

One way to keep cool on a hot, summer day is to wear light-colored clothes.

HERE'S WHAT YOU WILL DO

Reset or shake down both thermometers. Wrap the white fabric around the bulb end of one thermometer with the fuzzy side out. Tape the fabric snugly in place. Do the same with the black fabric on the second thermometer.

Place the thermometers in a sunny, wind-free spot. Check the temperature on each thermometer after 20 minutes and again after an hour. Which thermometer's temperature increased more? Did the difference become greater over time?

HERE'S WHAT'S HAPPENING

People tend to wear light-colored clothing in summer and dark-colored clothing in winter. There's a very good reason for that. Dark colors absorb more light than they reflect. Light colors reflect more light than they absorb. Light is a form of energy that can change into a second form of energy—heat! So sunshine heats up dark fabrics and furs more than it does light fabrics and furs. That's why light-colored clothing feels more comfortable than dark clothes in hot, sunny weather.

INVISIBLE INK

IN THIS TWO-PART EXPERIMENT, YOU'LL MAKE TWO KINDS OF INVISIBLE INK AND LEARN HOW TO CREATE AND REVEAL HIDDEN MESSAGES.

YOU WILL NEED

- ❑ cotton swabs
- ❑ lemon juice
- ❑ white paper
- ❑ lamp with an incandescent (heat producing) bulb
- ❑ water
- ❑ baking soda
- ❑ purple grape juice

**TIME:
1 HOUR**

Ultraviolet (UV) light is one way to reveal fingerprints or a stamp with invisible ink on someone's hand.

MESS FACTOR:
2

Safety First!
Don't touch the paper or your fingers to the hot bulb!

HERE'S WHAT YOU WILL DO

1 For your first invisible message, dip a cotton swab into lemon juice and trace a secret word on a piece of paper.

2 Once the word written in lemon juice dries, have a friend hold the paper close to a switched-on lightbulb.

COOL FACT!

Throughout written history, hidden communications have been sent using invisible ink. One of the earliest methods used milk to write messages on paper. When the paper was dusted with soot and the soot was blown off, the message could be read.

HERE'S WHAT'S HAPPENING

What seems like magic is simple chemistry. The heat of the bulb causes the acid in the juice to react with oxygen in the air. This oxidation reaction turns the lemon juice brown. *Voila!* Your message appears!

"IN THE KNOW"

Research is going on to develop high-tech printers that use invisible ink. Such printers could put an invisible image on paper money. Using a special type of microscope, the hidden image could be seen—or not—to prove that the money is real, and not counterfeit.

HERE'S WHAT YOU WILL DO

For your second invisible ink, mix equal parts water and baking soda. Use your cotton-swab "pen" to write another secret word. Tell your friend to reveal the message by lightly swabbing the paper with purple grape juice.

HERE'S WHAT'S HAPPENING

By mixing baking soda and water, you created a base solution. The base "ink" neutralized the acid in the grape juice, turning the juice from purple to pink. So your message showed up as light letters on a dark background.

I think you're cool!

MAGIC CABBAGE ACID TEST

IN THIS EXPERIMENT, YOU'RE GOING TO MAKE YOUR OWN pH INDICATOR. AND YOU'LL TEST SUBSTANCES TO FIND OUT WHETHER THEY'RE ACIDS, BASES, OR NEUTRAL.

YOU WILL NEED

- ❏ fresh red cabbage
- ❏ small saucepan
- ❏ chopping knife
- ❏ spouted measuring cup
- ❏ 8 small, clear jars or plastic cups
- ❏ tap water, distilled water, lemon juice, baking soda, dish detergent, vinegar, cream of tartar, mashed fruit
- ❏ apron
- ❏ strainer
- ❏ spoon

 **TIME: 1 HOUR**

HERE'S WHAT YOU WILL DO

1 Ask an adult to help you chop about 1 cup of red cabbage into small pieces. Place in a saucepan and cover with water.

 ADULT

 MESS FACTOR: 4

⚠️ **Safety First!**
Very acid or very base substances are dangerous and can burn skin and eyes. Examples include battery acid and bleach. Do not use very acid or very base substances for this experiment. In this safe experiment, you'll be using weak acids and bases.

2 Gently boil the cabbage until the water turns purple. Turn off the heat and allow the water to cool. Pour the cabbage water through the strainer and into the spouted measuring cup. Fill each small jar with a couple of inches of cabbage water. (It's going to stink!)

3 Add a squirt or spoonful of a different test substance to each jar, and observe any color change.

IS IT AN ACID OR A BASE?

aciD = reD
Base = Blue

The color-changing strips above are called pH indicators. They measure the strength of acids and bases. When the strip is dipped into a solution, the strip changes color according to the solution's pH.

The blossom color of the hydrangea plant at left depends on the pH of the soil. In acid soil, the flowers are shades of blue. In base soil, the flowers will bloom in shades of pink.

HERE'S WHAT'S HAPPENING

tap water   distilled water   baking soda   dish detergent

cream of tartar   lemon juice   vinegar   mashed fruit

Chemists use a substance called an indicator to test if something is an acid or a base. The indicator changes color when acids or bases are added to it. In this experiment, the cabbage water is the indicator. Acids (such as cream of tartar, lemon juice, vinegar, and mashed fruit) turn the cabbage water red or pink.

Bases (such as baking soda and dish detergent) turn the cabbage water blue or green. A neutral substance (such as distilled water) doesn't change the color of the cabbage water. The cabbage water indicator for tap water changes color according to the minerals found in your tap water.

RADICAL RAINBOWS

RAINBOWS ARE AMONG THE GREATEST SHOWS IN NATURE IN THIS EXPERIMENT, YOU'LL CREATE AN INDOOR RAINBOW AND DEMONSTRATE THE SCIENCE BEHIND THIS FANTASTIC COLOR DISPLAY.

YOU WILL NEED

- water
- shallow baking dish
- mirror
- flashlight
- white cardboard
- modeling clay (optional)

TIME:
10 MINUTES

Rainbows form when the Sun shines through water droplets in the air.

MESS FACTOR:
1

HERE'S WHAT YOU WILL DO

1 Pour enough water into the baking dish to fill it half way.

2 Lean one edge of the mirror in the water at one end of the baking dish. The mirror should be positioned at a slight upward-pointing angle. If you find that the mirror doesn't stay put, just use some modeling clay to secure the mirror to your work surface.

3 Dim the lights in your room. (It doesn't have to be completely dark.) With one hand, shine your flashlight at the part of the mirror beneath the water's surface. With your other hand, hold the cardboard above the dish so that the cardboard catches the light reflected from the mirror. You may need to move the mirror, flashlight, and cardboard a bit to catch the rainbow.

COOL FACT!

Rainbows can be seen in various places when the Sun is behind you—in the sky just after it rains, in the mist of a waterfall, or even in the spray from a garden hose. Rainbows cannot be seen on cloudy days or when the air is very dry. This is because sunlight and drops of moisture in the air are needed for rainbows to form.

When Sun and Rain Meet

When a ray of light enters a raindrop at just the right angle, the light splits before being reflected back out of the droplet. The rays of separated color then strike your eyes to create the vision of a rainbow.

HERE'S WHAT'S HAPPENING

Rainbows appear when **airborne** water droplets split a ray of sunlight into the colors that make up **white light**. In nature, the appearance of a rainbow depends on the right combination of sunlight and rain or mist. In this experiment, the water and mirror are playing the role of raindrops, and your flashlight is the Sun. The mirror **reflects** the light from the flashlight, which passes back through the water, traveling at an angle. The water **refracts**, or bends, the light. As the light bends, it separates into all the colors that make up white light: red, orange, yellow, green, blue, indigo, and violet. When you hold the flashlight just right, a rainbow appears on the cardboard!

CREEPING COLORS

HAVE YOU EVER WONDERED HOW WATER MOVES THROUGH PLANT STEMS? IN THIS EXPERIMENT, YOU'LL USE FOOD COLORING TO SHOW HOW PLANTS "DRINK" THROUGH SPECIAL TUBES CALLED XYLEM.

YOU WILL NEED

- ❑ 4 small glasses
- ❑ water
- ❑ food coloring (2 different colors)
- ❑ scissors
- ❑ white carnation (fresh)
- ❑ celery stalk (fresh)

TIME: 2 DAYS

MESS FACTOR: 4

⚠️ **Caution!**
Food coloring can stain your clothes and work surface. Be sure to wear an apron or an old shirt, and cover your work space with newspaper.

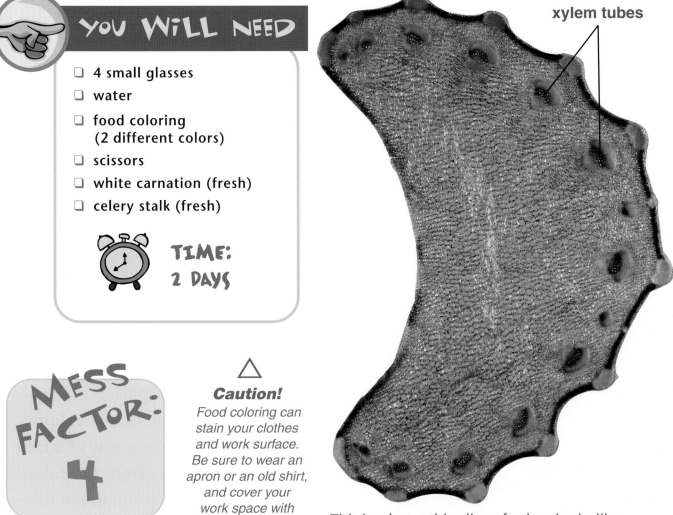

xylem tubes

This is what a thin slice of celery looks like under a microscope. The little oval spots are the xylem tubes.

HERE'S WHAT YOU WILL DO

1 Fill your glasses half full of water. Add a big squirt of food coloring to two of the glasses. Choose a different color, and do the same with the other two glasses of water.

2 Cut an inch off the bottom of the carnation stem and the celery stalk. With the scissors, split both the stem and the stalk up the middle, cutting several inches up from the bottom toward the flower or leaves.

3 Place each half of the carnation stem in a differen glass with different colored water. Do the same with the celery stalk. Let them sit for a day or two. How d they look? Both the carnation and the celery stalk should be tinted half one color and half the other.

HERE'S WHAT'S HAPPENING

Plants move water and nutrients up through the outside layer of their stalks, stems, or trunks with special tubes called xylem. In this experiment, the colored water that travels up one side of a split stem remains separate from the colored water that travels up through the other side. That's how you end up with a two-toned flower or leaf at the top!

BENDING LIGHT

IN THESE EXPERIMENTS, YOU'LL SEE A COLORFUL EFFECT OF REFRACTION AND AN OPTICAL ILLUSION AS LIGHT PASSES FROM ONE TRANSPARENT SUBSTANCE INTO ANOTHER.

YOU WILL NEED

- ❑ colored plastic wrap
- ❑ cardboard
- ❑ scissors
- ❑ flashlight
- ❑ tape
- ❑ clear glass bowl
- ❑ water
- ❑ milk
- ❑ drinking glass
- ❑ long spoon

TIME: 30 MINUTES

MESS FACTOR: 1

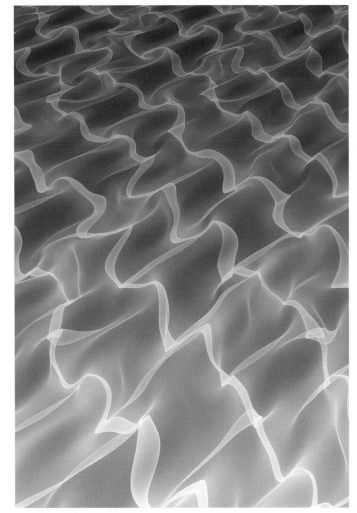

When rays of light hit the surface of a swimming pool, the rippling water bends the light into all sorts of unusual patterns.

HERE'S WHAT YOU WILL DO

1

Cover the front of the flashlight with a piece of colored plastic wrap. Cut a piece of cardboard to a size you can tape over the plastic wrap and around the edge of the flashlight. In the middle of the cardboard, cut a slit that's almost the length of the flashlight lens and about the width of a pencil. Tape the cardboard over the front of the flashlight.

2

Fill the bowl two-thirds with water, add several drops of milk, and stir. Turn off the lights (the room doesn't have to be pitch-dark), and shine the flashlight into the bowl at an angle. Follow the path of the beam as it passes through the air and into the slightly milky water. Can you see it zigzag?

HERE'S WHAT'S HAPPENING

Light passes more slowly through water than through air. This change in speed causes refraction, which is the bending of light as it passes from the air into the water.

3 Turn the lights back on, and fill the drinking glass nearly to the top with water. Place the stem of the spoon straight down into the water. Keeping the spoon straight up and down, look at the stem though the side of the glass. It looks straight, right?

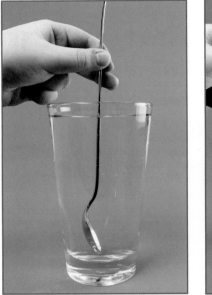

Now tilt the spoon so its stem rests on one lip of the glass. Look at the spoon through the side of the glass. What do you see? The spoon appears bent! **4**

HERE'S WHAT'S HAPPENING

Imagine an invisible line running straight up and down between you and the glass of water. Light from the spoon bends away from this line as it travels out of the water and into the air on its way to your eyes. If the spoon stem is at an angle to the line, this bending produces the optical illusion of a zig-zag at the water's surface. If the spoon stem is straight up and down, the light bends out from the line equally in both directions. So the part of the spoon below the water appears a little wider than it really is. But it remains in line with the part of the spoon above the water.

ANIMAL COVER-UP

IN THIS EXPERIMENT, YOU'LL SEE HOW NATURE PROTECTS THE EGGS OF GROUND-DWELLING BIRDS BY COVERING THEM IN CAMOUFLAGE. AND YOU'LL MAKE YOUR OWN CAMOUFLAGED EGG.

YOU WILL NEED

- ☐ 2 white hard-boiled eggs
- ☐ brown & black markers
- ☐ dirt
- ☐ dry leaves
- ☐ small sticks
- ☐ other natural materials

TIME: 30 MINUTES

MESS FACTOR: 3

This mother quail watches over her eggs. The bird's feathers and the color of the eggs blend with the surroundings, helping to hide them from predators.

HERE'S WHAT YOU WILL DO

1 Make one of your eggs look like a quail egg in the picture on page 24 by adding speckles with your markers. Then rub the egg all over with some dry dirt. Leave the other egg white.

2 Make two nests of about the same size and shape with your natural materials. Place one egg in each nest.

3 Now walk a few feet away and look back at the nests. Which egg is easier to spot?

HERE'S WHAT'S HAPPENING

Squirrels, skunks, hawks, and other predators like nothing better than a tasty meal of eggs! That's bad news for the eggs of ground-dwelling birds such as quail and grouse. But nature protects these eggs with camouflage—a light brown shell and speckled markings—to help them blend in with their surroundings and stay hidden from predators.

HiDDEN HUES

WHAT'S INSIDE A COLOR? SOMETIMES LOTS OF OTHER COLORS! IN THIS EXPERIMENT, UNCOVER CLUES TO HIDDEN HUES.

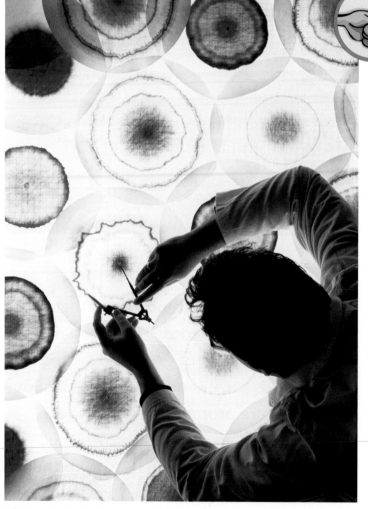

This scientist is measuring how far a color has spread on a piece of filter paper.

YOU WiLL NEED

- ❏ white coffee filters
- ❏ scissors
- ❏ 4 saucers
- ❏ water
- ❏ 2 different brands of black "washable" markers
- ❏ colored candy pieces, like M&Ms or Runts

TIME: 30 MINUTES

MESS FACTOR: 4

HERE'S WHAT YOU WILL DO

1 Cut the coffee filters into strips about an inch wide and several inches long.

2 Fill the center of a saucer with lukewarm water. Use one marker to draw a large dot an inch above the bottom edge of a filter strip. Use the other brand of marker to do the same on another strip.

3 Place the bottom edge of the strips into the saucer. Watch as the colors in the ink crawl up the paper and separate. Do some colors move faster or farther than others? Do the different brands of black ink contain the same colors?

A SWEET VARIATION

1 Fill the center of each saucer with lukewarm water, and add several candies of one color. After a few minutes, turn the candies over so more color bleeds into the water.

2 Place one end of a filter strip into each saucer of candy-colored water. Which colors separate into other colors? Which stay the same? Those that don't separate are primary colors. Those that do separate are secondary colors, or mixtures.

HERE'S WHAT'S HAPPENING

In this experiment, you are practicing the science of chromatography—separating parts of a mixture by letting it travel through a material that absorbs each part at a different rate.

As the water is soaked up by the filter paper, it carries the color in the inks and in the candies with it. You'll notice that different pigments travel through the paper at different speeds. The chemicals in the inks and dyes slowly separate, making colorful patterns. Black ink can contain all the colors of the rainbow. Even the bright colors of the candies can be made up of several primary colors.

FIND OUT MORE

For more information on the science of color, check out these books and Web sites:

BOOKS

Doherty, Paul, and Don Rathjen. *The Magic Wand and Other Bright Experiments on Light and Color.* John Wiley & Sons, 1995.

Hewitt, Sally. *It's Science: Hot and Cold.* Scholastic, 2000.

Krupp, E.C. *The Rainbow and You.* Harper-Collins, 2000.

Kuehni, Rolf. *Color.* Wiley, 2004.

Levine, Shar, and Leslie Johnstone. *The Optics Book: Fun Experiments with Light, Vision, and Color.* Sterling, 1999.

Richards, Jon. *Chemicals and Reactions.* Millbrook/Cooper Beach, 2000.

Riley, Peter. *Light and Color.* Franklin Watts, 1999.

Silverstein, Alvin; Virginia B. Silverstein; and Laura Silverstein Nunn. *Creepy Crawlies.* Millbrook Press, 2003.

Tomecek, Steve. *Bouncing and Bending Light: Phantastic Physical Phenomena.* Freeman, 1995.

WEB SITES

Acids, Alkalis and Neutralization
www.bgfl.org/bgfl/custom/resources_ftp/client_ftp/ks3/science/acids/
These animated activities illustrate litmus testing, universal indicator reactions, and neutralization. From Birmingham Grid for Learning, an educational resource for schools of the city of Birmingham, England. (Plug-ins required.)

Eek! Critter Corner
www.dnr.state.wi.us/org/caer/ce/eek/critter/insect/index.htm
Learn about beetles, bees, butterflies, and other bugs from EEK! (Environmental Education for Kids), an electronic magazine published by the Wisconsin Department of Natural Resources.

Living Colour
www.amonline.net.au/colour/
What is color? Is it our eyes or our brains that actually see color? How do some animals produce glow-in-the-dark colors? Have all your color questions answered at the Living Colour site from the Australian Museum in Sydney.

Rainbow Activity
acept.la.asu.edu/PiN/act/rainbow/rainbow.shtml
Find out how and why rainbows form, and learn how to create your own rainbows at home. From the Department of Physics and Astronomy, Arizona State University.

WonderNet—Heat
www.chemistry.org/portal/Chemistry?PID=wondernetdisplay.html&DOC=wondernet\activities\heat\heat.html
If you're looking for a place to learn about heat, you're getting warmer. Try the fun activities at this WonderNet site to discover interesting things about heat. From the American Chemical Society.

GLOSSARY

A

absorb to soak up or take in.

acids substances that will react with a base to form a salt. Examples of acid substances are lemon juice and vinegar.

airborne carried by or through the air.

B

bases substances that will react with an acid to form a salt. Examples of base substances are ammonia and dish detergent.

C

camouflage coloring or covering that makes animals, people, and objects look like their surroundings.

chemicals substances produced by or used in chemistry.

chemistry the scientific study of substances, what they are composed of, and the ways in which they react with each other.

chromatography the process of separating parts of a mixture by letting it travel through a material that absorbs each part at a different rate.

coax to persuade by gentle and patient urging.

counterfeit something that has been made to look like the real thing but is a fake.

E

energy power, or the ability to make something change or move. Forms of energy include light, heat, and electricity.

I

insects small animals with three main body parts, three pairs of legs, one pair of antennae, and (usually) two sets of wings

N

nectar a sweet liquid that bees collect from flowers and turn into honey.

neutral being neither an acid nor a base.

neutralized stopped something from working or from having an effect.

nutrients something that is needed by people, animals, and plants to stay strong and healthy.

O

optical illusion something that you think you see that is not really there.

oxidation the process of reacting with oxygen in the air or water.

P

pH a scale of 1 to 14, from extreme acid (1) to extreme base (14). Something with a pH of 7 is "neutral." The initials pH stand for **p**otential of **H**ydrogen.

pigments substances that give color to something.

pollen tiny yellow grains produced in the anthers, or male parts, of flowers.

pollination the transfer of pollen from the male part of a flower to the female part of a flower.

predators animals that live by hunting other animals for food.

primary colors the pure colors from which all other colors are made. Red, yellow, and blue are the primary colors in inks and other colorings. Red, blue, and green are the primary colors in light.

R

rays narrow beams of light or other radiation.

reflects sends back light rays, heat, or sound from a surface.

refraction the bending of light as it passes from one clear substance into another of a different density.

S

secondary colors the colors formed by mixing two primary colors in equal quantities.

T

transparent allowing light to pass through so that objects on the other side can be seen clearly.

W

white light light that is a mixture of wavelengths of various colors and is perceived as colorless, such as sunlight.

X

xylem the water-conducting tissue of a plant.

 INDEX

Pictures are shown in **bold**.

Photographs © 2008: age fotostock/Bartomeu Borrel 3 top left, 5 center, 6; Animals Animals/Robert Maier 5 right, 24; Corbis Images: 4 right center, 14 left (Darrell Gulin), 10 (Vic Yepello/Star Ledger); Getty Images: 8 (Andreanna Seymore), 16 (Joseph Van Os); Photo Researchers, NY: 14 right (Gusto), 3 right center, 21 (Eric Heller), 19 (Oliver Meckes/Nicole Ottawa), 3 bottom right, 5 left, 26 (G. Tompkinson); Richard Hutchings Photography: cover, back cover, 1, 3 left center, 3 top right, 4 left center, 4 left, 5 right center, 5 left center, 7, 9 top, 9 bottom, 11, 12, 13, 15, 18, 20 top, 20 bottom, 22, 23 left, 23 right, 25 top, 25 bottom, 27 right, 27 left, 28.